# Succeeding On Purpose 2021 Planner

## By Dr. Denise Johnson

Copyright © 2020 Denise Johnson

ALL RIGHTS RESERVED. This book contains material protected under International and Federal Copyright Laws and Treaties. Any unauthorized reprint or use of this material is prohibited. No part of this book may be reproduced or transmitted in any form or by any means, electronic or mechanical, including photocopying, recording, or by any information storage and retrieval system without express written permission from the author/publisher.

Publishing Services:
www.legacydrivenconsulting.com

## Hello Friend!

Congratulations for purchasing this Planner!
As you embrace this new season; it is my prayer that you will "Succeed On Purpose".
This planner will be a blessing to you.

Kingdom blessings!

### Dr. Denise Johnson

# 2021

## January
| M | T | W | T | F | S | S |
|---|---|---|---|---|---|---|
|   |   |   |   | 1 | 2 | 3 |
| 4 | 5 | 6 | 7 | 8 | 9 | 10 |
| 11 | 12 | 13 | 14 | 15 | 16 | 17 |
| 18 | 19 | 20 | 21 | 22 | 23 | 24 |
| 25 | 26 | 27 | 28 | 29 | 30 | 31 |

## February
| M | T | W | T | F | S | S |
|---|---|---|---|---|---|---|
| 1 | 2 | 3 | 4 | 5 | 6 | 7 |
| 8 | 9 | 10 | 11 | 12 | 13 | 14 |
| 15 | 16 | 17 | 18 | 19 | 20 | 21 |
| 22 | 23 | 24 | 25 | 26 | 27 | 28 |

## March
| M | T | W | T | F | S | S |
|---|---|---|---|---|---|---|
| 1 | 2 | 3 | 4 | 5 | 6 | 7 |
| 8 | 9 | 10 | 11 | 12 | 13 | 14 |
| 15 | 16 | 17 | 18 | 19 | 20 | 21 |
| 22 | 23 | 24 | 25 | 26 | 27 | 28 |
| 29 | 30 | 31 |   |   |   |   |

## April
| M | T | W | T | F | S | S |
|---|---|---|---|---|---|---|
|   |   |   | 1 | 2 | 3 | 4 |
| 5 | 6 | 77 | 8 | 9 | 10 | 11 |
| 12 | 13 | 14 | 15 | 16 | 17 | 18 |
| 19 | 20 | 21 | 22 | 23 | 24 | 25 |
| 26 | 27 | 28 | 29 | 30 |   |   |

## May
| M | T | W | T | F | S | S |
|---|---|---|---|---|---|---|
|   |   |   |   |   | 1 | 2 |
| 3 | 4 | 5 | 6 | 7 | 8 | 9 |
| 10 | 11 | 12 | 13 | 14 | 15 | 16 |
| 17 | 18 | 19 | 20 | 21 | 22 | 23 |
| 24 | 25 | 26 | 27 | 28 | 29 | 30 |
| 31 |   |   |   |   |   |   |

## June
| M | T | W | T | F | S | S |
|---|---|---|---|---|---|---|
|   | 1 | 2 | 3 | 4 | 5 | 6 |
| 7 | 8 | 9 | 10 | 11 | 12 | 13 |
| 14 | 15 | 16 | 17 | 18 | 19 | 20 |
| 21 | 22 | 23 | 24 | 25 | 26 | 27 |
| 28 | 29 | 30 |   |   |   |   |

## July
| M | T | W | T | F | S | S |
|---|---|---|---|---|---|---|
|   |   |   | 1 | 2 | 3 | 4 |
| 5 | 6 | 7 | 8 | 9 | 10 | 11 |
| 12 | 13 | 14 | 15 | 16 | 17 | 18 |
| 19 | 20 | 21 | 22 | 23 | 24 | 25 |
| 26 | 27 | 28 | 29 | 30 | 31 |   |

## August
| M | T | W | T | F | S | S |
|---|---|---|---|---|---|---|
|   |   |   |   |   |   | 1 |
| 2 | 3 | 4 | 5 | 6 | 7 | 8 |
| 9 | 10 | 11 | 12 | 13 | 14 | 15 |
| 16 | 17 | 18 | 19 | 20 | 21 | 22 |
| 23 | 24 | 25 | 26 | 27 | 28 | 29 |
| 30 | 31 |   |   |   |   |   |

## September
| M | T | W | T | F | S | S |
|---|---|---|---|---|---|---|
|   |   | 1 | 2 | 3 | 4 | 5 |
| 6 | 7 | 8 | 9 | 10 | 11 | 12 |
| 13 | 14 | 15 | 16 | 17 | 18 | 19 |
| 20 | 21 | 22 | 23 | 24 | 25 | 26 |
| 27 | 28 | 29 | 30 |   |   |   |

## October
| M | T | W | T | F | S | S |
|---|---|---|---|---|---|---|
|   |   |   |   | 1 | 2 | 3 |
| 4 | 5 | 6 | 7 | 8 | 9 | 10 |
| 11 | 12 | 13 | 14 | 15 | 16 | 17 |
| 18 | 19 | 20 | 21 | 22 | 23 | 24 |
| 25 | 26 | 27 | 28 | 29 | 30 | 31 |

## November
| M | T | W | T | F | S | S |
|---|---|---|---|---|---|---|
| 1 | 2 | 3 | 4 | 5 | 6 | 7 |
| 8 | 9 | 10 | 11 | 12 | 13 | 14 |
| 15 | 16 | 17 | 18 | 19 | 20 | 21 |
| 22 | 23 | 24 | 25 | 26 | 27 | 28 |
| 29 | 30 |   |   |   |   |   |

## December
| M | T | W | T | F | S | S |
|---|---|---|---|---|---|---|
|   |   | 1 | 2 | 3 | 4 | 5 |
| 6 | 7 | 8 | 9 | 10 | 11 | 12 |
| 13 | 14 | 15 | 116 | 17 | 18 | 19 |
| 20 | 21 | 22 | 23 | 24 | 25 | 26 |
| 27 | 28 | 29 | 30 | 31 |   |   |

# Holidays & Observances

## January
1 New Year's Day
6 Epiphany
10 Majority Rule Day
11 Majority Rule Day Holiday
18 Martin Luther King Day

## February
2 Groundhog Day
12 Chinese New Year
12 Lincoln's Birthday
14 Valentine's Day
15 President's Day
17 Ash Wednesday

## March
14 Daylight Savings
17 St. Patrick's Day
20 Vernal Equinox
28 Passover

## April
1 April Fool's day
2 Good Friday
4 Easter
13 Ramadan Begins
15 Taxes Due
21 Admin Assistant's Day

## May
5 Cinco de Mayo
9 Mother's Day
13 Ascension Day
23 Pentecost
24 Whit Monday
31 Memorial Day

## June
4 Sir Randolph Fawkes Day
14 Flag Day
20 Father's Day
21 June Solstice

## July
10 Independence Day
25 Parents' Day

## August
2 Emancipation Day
7 Purple Heart Day
15 Assumption of Mary
26 Woman's Equality

## September
6 Labor Day
7 Rosh Hashanah
12 Grandparents Day
22 Autumnal Equinox

## October
11 National Heroes Day
16 Boss's Day
31 Halloween

## November
7 Daylight Savings
11 Veterans' Day
25 Thanksgiving
28 Hanukkah Begins

## December
21 December Solstice
25 Christmas Day
26 Kwanzaa Begins
31 New Year's Eve

# 2021

## Goals

## Resolutions

I can do all things through *Christ* who strengthens me. *Philippians 4:13*

# January

| Monday | Tuesday | Wednesday | Thursday | Friday | Saturday | Sunday |
|---|---|---|---|---|---|---|
|  |  |  |  | 1 | 2 | 3 |
| 4 | 5 | 6 | 7 | 8 | 9 | 10 |
| 11 | 12 | 13 | 14 | 15 | 16 | 17 |
| 18 | 19 | 20 | 21 | 22 | 23 | 24 |
| 25 | 26 | 27 | 28 | 29 | 30 | 31 |

And my *God* will meet all your needs according to his glorious riches in *Christ Jesus.* Philippians 4:19

Item:  Due Date:  Complete

# January Budget

## Income

| | Projected | Actual |
|---|---|---|
| Salary | | |
| Income 2 | | |
| Income 3 | | |
| Totals: | | |

## Personal

| | Projected | Actual |
|---|---|---|
| Personal Loans | | |
| Credit Cards | | |
| Retirement Plan | | |
| Savings Plan | | |
| Health Ins. | | |
| Life & Nat. Ins. | | |
| Groceries/Food | | |
| Investments | | |
| Clothing/Cleaning | | |
| Entertainment | | |
| Vacation | | |
| Other | | |
| Totals: | | |

## Expenses

### Gifts & Donations

| | Projected | Actual |
|---|---|---|
| Tithes | | |
| Offerings | | |
| Charity | | |
| Other | | |
| Totals: | | |

### Housing

| | Projected | Actual |
|---|---|---|
| Mortage/Rent | | |
| Maint./Repairs | | |
| Phone/Internet | | |
| BPL | | |
| Water & Sew.. | | |
| Propane Gas | | |
| Home Ins. | | |
| Real Prop. Tax | | |
| Other | | |
| Totals: | | |

### Transportation

| | Projected | Actual |
|---|---|---|
| Vehicle/Transport | | |
| Car Insurance | | |
| Car Licensing | | |
| Car Maint. | | |
| Fuel Cost | | |
| Other | | |
| Totals: | | |

### Total Expenses

| | Projected | Actual |
|---|---|---|
| Total Expenses: | | |

## 28 December - 3 January
# Week 1

**Weekly List of Priorities:**

**Monday**

**Tuesday**

**Wednesday**

**Thursday**

**Friday**

**Saturday**

**Sunday**

# 28 December - 3 January
# Week 1 Finance Record

| Income | Total |
|---|---|
| Salary or Commissions | |
| Supplemental Income | |
| Sub Total | |

| Investments | Total |
|---|---|
| Tithes, Offerings, Seeds | |
| Investment Portfolio | |
| Savings Plan / Asue | |
| Sub Total | |

| Expenditures | Total |
|---|---|
| Mortage/Rent/Utilities | |
| Health, Life & National Ins. | |
| Auto Fuel and Maintenance | |
| Loans, Retirement & Vacations | |
| Entertainment/Clothing | |
| Groceries/Food | |
| Others | |
| Sub Total | |

Weekly Surplus/Deficit Total: _____

Observations: _____

Changes: _____

# 4 January - 10 January
## Week 2

Weekly List of Priorities:

**Monday**

**Tuesday**

**Wednesday**

**Thursday**

**Friday**

**Saturday**

**Sunday**

## 4 January - 10 January
# Week 2 Finance Record

| *Income* | *Total* |
|---|---|
| Salary or Commissions | |
| Supplemental Income | |
| Sub Total | |
| *Investments* | *Total* |
| Tithes, Offerings, Seeds | |
| Investment Portfolio | |
| Savings Plan / Asue | |
| Sub Total | |
| *Expenditures* | *Total* |
| Mortage/Rent/Utilities | |
| Health, Life & National Ins. | |
| Auto Fuel and Maintenance | |
| Loans, Retirement & Vacations | |
| Entertainment/Clothing | |
| Groceries/Food | |
| Others | |
| Sub Total | |

Weekly Surplus/Deficit Total: _____

Observations: _____

_____

Changes: _____

_____

## 11 January - 17 January
# Week 3

**Weekly List of Priorities:**

### Monday

### Tuesday

### Wednesday

### Thursday

### Friday

### Saturday

### Sunday

# 11 January - 17 January
# Week 3 Finance Record

| Income | Total |
|---|---|
| Salary or Commissions | |
| Supplemental Income | |
| Sub Total | |

| Investments | Total |
|---|---|
| Tithes, Offerings, Seeds | |
| Investment Portfolio | |
| Savings Plan / Asue | |
| Sub Total | |

| Expenditures | Total |
|---|---|
| Mortage/Rent/Utilities | |
| Health, Life & National Ins. | |
| Auto Fuel and Maintenance | |
| Loans, Retirement & Vacations | |
| Entertainment/Clothing | |
| Groceries/Food | |
| Others | |
| Sub Total | |

Weekly Surplus/Deficit Total: _____

Observations: _____

Changes: _____

18 January - 24 January
# Week 4

Weekly List of Priorities:

*Monday*

*Tuesday*

*Wednesday*

*Thursday*

*Friday*

*Saturday*

*Sunday*

# 18 January - 24 January
# Week 4 Finance Record

| Income | Total |
|---|---|
| Salary or Commissions | |
| Supplemental Income | |
| Sub Total | |

| Investments | Total |
|---|---|
| Tithes, Offerings, Seeds | |
| Investment Portfolio | |
| Savings Plan / Asue | |
| Sub Total | |

| Expenditures | Total |
|---|---|
| Mortage/Rent/Utilities | |
| Health, Life & National Ins. | |
| Auto Fuel and Maintenance | |
| Loans, Retirement & Vacations | |
| Entertainment/Clothing | |
| Groceries/Food | |
| Others | |
| Sub Total | |

Weekly Surplus/Deficit Total: _____

Observations: _____

_____

Changes: _____

_____

25 January - 31 January
# Week 5

Weekly List of Priorities:

- Monday
- Tuesday
- Wednesday
- Thursday
- Friday
- Saturday
- Sunday

# 25 January - 31 January
# Week 5 Finance Record

| Income | Total |
|---|---|
| Salary or Commissions | |
| Supplemental Income | |
| Sub Total | |
| **Investments** | **Total** |
| Tithes, Offerings, Seeds | |
| Investment Portfolio | |
| Savings Plan / Asue | |
| Sub Total | |
| **Expenditures** | **Total** |
| Mortage/Rent/Utilities | |
| Health, Life & National Ins. | |
| Auto Fuel and Maintenance | |
| Loans, Retirement & Vacations | |
| Entertainment/Clothing | |
| Groceries/Food | |
| Others | |
| Sub Total | |

Weekly Surplus/Deficit Total: _____

Observations: _____

_____

Changes: _____

# January Review

## Achieved

## What can I do better?

Notes:

# February

| Monday | Tuesday | Wednesday | Thursday | Friday | Saturday | Sunday |
|---|---|---|---|---|---|---|
| 1 | 2 | 3 | 4 | 5 | 6 | 7 |
| 8 | 9 | 10 | 11 | 12 | 13 | 14 |
| 15 | 16 | 17 | 18 | 19 | 20 | 21 |
| 22 | 23 | 24 | 25 | 26 | 27 | 28 |

'Honor the *Lord* with your wealth, with the first fruits of all your crops; then your barns will be filled to overflowing, and your vats will brim over with new wine.'

*Proverbs 3:9-10*

## To-do List

Item:            Due Date:        Complete

# February Budget

## Income

| | Projected | Actual |
|---|---|---|
| Salary | | |
| Income 2 | | |
| Income 3 | | |
| Totals: | | |

## Personal

| | Projected | Actual |
|---|---|---|
| Personal Loans | | |
| Credit Cards | | |
| Retirement Plan | | |
| Savings Plan | | |
| Health Ins. | | |
| Life & Nat. Ins. | | |
| Groceries/Food | | |
| Investments | | |
| Clothing/Cleaning | | |
| Entertainment | | |
| Vacation | | |
| Other | | |
| Totals: | | |

## Expenses

### Gifts & Donations

| | Projected | Actual |
|---|---|---|
| Tithes | | |
| Offerings | | |
| Charity | | |
| Other | | |
| Totals: | | |

### Housing

| | Projected | Actual |
|---|---|---|
| Mortage/Rent | | |
| Maint./Repairs | | |
| Phone/Internet | | |
| BPL | | |
| Water & Sew. | | |
| Propane Gas | | |
| Home Ins. | | |
| Real Prop. Tax | | |
| Other | | |
| Totals: | | |

### Transportation

| | Projected | Actual |
|---|---|---|
| Vehicle/Transport | | |
| Car Insurance | | |
| Car Licensing | | |
| Car Maint. | | |
| Fuel Cost | | |
| Other | | |
| Totals: | | |

## Total Expenses

| | Projected | Actual |
|---|---|---|
| Total Expenses: | | |

# Week 6
*1 February - 7 February*

Weekly List of Priorities:

- Monday
- Tuesday
- Wednesday
- Thursday
- Friday
- Saturday
- Sunday

*1 February - 7 February*
# Week 6 Finance Record

| Income | Total |
|---|---|
| Salary or Commissions | |
| Supplemental Income | |
| Sub Total | |

| Investments | Total |
|---|---|
| Tithes, Offerings, Seeds | |
| Investment Portfolio | |
| Savings Plan / Asue | |
| Sub Total | |

| Expenditures | Total |
|---|---|
| Mortage/Rent/Utilities | |
| Health, Life & National Ins. | |
| Auto Fuel and Maintenance | |
| Loans, Retirement & Vacations | |
| Entertainment/Clothing | |
| Groceries/Food | |
| Others | |
| Sub Total | |

Weekly Surplus/Deficit Total: _____

Observations: _____

Changes: _____

*8 February - 14 February*
# Week 7

Weekly List of Priorities:

**Monday**

**Tuesday**

**Wednesday**

**Thursday**

**Friday**

**Saturday**

**Sunday**

*8 February - 14 February*
# Week 7 Finance Record

| *Income* | *Total* |
|---|---|
| Salary or Commissions | |
| Supplemental Income | |
| Sub Total | |
| *Investments* | *Total* |
| Tithes, Offerings, Seeds | |
| Investment Portfolio | |
| Savings Plan / Asue | |
| Sub Total | |
| *Expenditures* | *Total* |
| Mortage/Rent/Utilities | |
| Health, Life & National Ins. | |
| Auto Fuel and Maintenance | |
| Loans, Retirement & Vacations | |
| Entertainment/Clothing | |
| Groceries/Food | |
| Others | |
| Sub Total | |

Weekly Surplus/Deficit Total: _____

Observations: _____

_____

Changes: _____

_____

# 15 February - 21 February
# Week 8

Weekly List of Priorities:

**Monday**

**Tuesday**

**Wednesday**

**Thursday**

**Friday**

**Saturday**

**Sunday**

# 15 February - 21 February
# Week 8 Finance Record

| Income | Total |
|---|---|
| Salary or Commissions | |
| Supplemental Income | |
| Sub Total | |大
| **Investments** | **Total** |
| Tithes, Offerings, Seeds | |
| Investment Portfolio | |
| Savings Plan / Asue | |
| Sub Total | |
| **Expenditures** | **Total** |
| Mortage/Rent/Utilities | |
| Health, Life & National Ins. | |
| Auto Fuel and Maintenance | |
| Loans, Retirement & Vacations | |
| Entertainment/Clothing | |
| Groceries/Food | |
| Others | |
| Sub Total | |

Weekly Surplus/Deficit Total: _____

Observations: _____

Changes: _____

# 22 February - 28 February
## Week 9

Weekly List of Priorities:

**Monday**

**Tuesday**

**Wednesday**

**Thursday**

**Friday**

**Saturday**

**Sunday**

## 22 February - 28 February
# Week 9 Finance Record

| Income | Total |
|---|---|
| Salary or Commissions | |
| Supplemental Income | |
| Sub Total | |

| Investments | Total |
|---|---|
| Tithes, Offerings, Seeds | |
| Investment Portfolio | |
| Savings Plan / Asue | |
| Sub Total | |

| Expenditures | Total |
|---|---|
| Mortage/Rent/Utilities | |
| Health, Life & National Ins. | |
| Auto Fuel and Maintenance | |
| Loans, Retirement & Vacations | |
| Entertainment/Clothing | |
| Groceries/Food | |
| Others | |
| Sub Total | |

Weekly Surplus/Deficit Total: _____

Observations: _____

_____

Changes: _____

_____

# February Review

## Achieved

## What can I do better?

Notes:

# March

| Monday | Tuesday | Wednesday | Thursday | Friday | Saturday | Sunday |
|--------|---------|-----------|----------|--------|----------|--------|
| 1 | 2 | 3 | 4 | 5 | 6 | 7 |
| 8 | 9 | 10 | 11 | 12 | 13 | 14 |
| 15 | 16 | 17 | 18 | 19 | 20 | 21 |
| 22 | 23 | 24 | 25 | 26 | 27 | 28 |
| 29 | 30 | 31 | | | | |

I returned, and saw under the sun, that the race is not to the swift, nor the battle to the strong, neither yet bread to the wise, nor yet riches to men of understanding, nor yet favour to men of skill; but time and chance happeneth to them all.

*Ecclesiastes 9:11*

# March
## To-do List

Item:    Due Date:    Complete

# March Budget

## Income

| | Projected | Actual |
|---|---|---|
| Salary | | |
| Income 2 | | |
| Income 3 | | |
| Totals: | | |

## Expenses

### Gifts & Donations

| | Projected | Actual |
|---|---|---|
| Tithes | | |
| Offerings | | |
| Charity | | |
| Other | | |
| Totals: | | |

### Housing

| | Projected | Actual |
|---|---|---|
| Mortage/Rent | | |
| Maint./Repairs | | |
| Phone/Internet | | |
| BPL | | |
| Water & Sew.. | | |
| Propane Gas | | |
| Home Ins. | | |
| Real Prop. Tax | | |
| Other | | |
| Totals: | | |

## Personal

| | Projected | Actual |
|---|---|---|
| Personal Loans | | |
| Credit Cards | | |
| Retirement Plan | | |
| Savings Plan | | |
| Health Ins. | | |
| Life & Nat. Ins. | | |
| Groceries/Food | | |
| Investments | | |
| Clothing/Cleaning | | |
| Entertainment | | |
| Vacation | | |
| Other | | |
| Totals: | | |

### Transportation

| | Projected | Actual |
|---|---|---|
| Vehicle/Transport | | |
| Car Insurance | | |
| Car Licensing | | |
| Car Maint. | | |
| Fuel Cost | | |
| Other | | |
| Totals: | | |

### Total Expenses

| | Projected | Actual |
|---|---|---|
| Total Expenses: | | |

*1 March - 7 March*
# Week 10

Weekly List of Priorities:

*Monday*

*Tuesday*

*Wednesday*

*Thursday*

*Friday*

*Saturday*

*Sunday*

# 1 March - 7 March
# Week 10 Finance Record

| *Income* | *Total* |
|---|---|
| Salary or Commissions | |
| Supplemental Income | |
| Sub Total | |

| *Investments* | *Total* |
|---|---|
| Tithes, Offerings, Seeds | |
| Investment Portfolio | |
| Savings Plan / Asue | |
| Sub Total | |

| *Expenditures* | *Total* |
|---|---|
| Mortage/Rent/Utilities | |
| Health, Life & National Ins. | |
| Auto Fuel and Maintenance | |
| Loans, Retirement & Vacations | |
| Entertainment/Clothing | |
| Groceries/Food | |
| Others | |
| Sub Total | |

Weekly Surplus/Deficit Total: _____

Observations: _____

Changes: _____

*8 March - 14 March*
# Week 11

Weekly List of Priorities:

- Monday
- Tuesday
- Wednesday
- Thursday
- Friday
- Saturday
- Sunday

*8 March - 14 March*
# Week 11 Finance Record

| Income | Total |
|---|---|
| Salary or Commissions | |
| Supplemental Income | |
| Sub Total | |
| *Investments* | Total |
| Tithes, Offerings, Seeds | |
| Investment Portfolio | |
| Savings Plan / Asue | |
| Sub Total | |
| *Expenditures* | Total |
| Mortage/Rent/Utilities | |
| Health, Life & National Ins. | |
| Auto Fuel and Maintenance | |
| Loans, Retirement & Vacations | |
| Entertainment/Clothing | |
| Groceries/Food | |
| Others | |
| Sub Total | |

Weekly Surplus/Deficit Total: _____

Observations: _____

_____

Changes: _____

_____

15 March - 21 March
# Week 12

Weekly List of Priorities:

**Monday**

**Tuesday**

**Wednesday**

**Thursday**

**Friday**

**Saturday**

**Sunday**

*15 March - 21 March*
# Week 12 Finance Record

| *Income* | *Total* |
|---|---|
| Salary or Commissions | |
| Supplemental Income | |
| Sub Total | |
| *Investments* | *Total* |
| Tithes, Offerings, Seeds | |
| Investment Portfolio | |
| Savings Plan / Asue | |
| Sub Total | |
| *Expenditures* | *Total* |
| Mortage/Rent/Utilities | |
| Health, Life & National Ins. | |
| Auto Fuel and Maintenance | |
| Loans, Retirement & Vacations | |
| Entertainment/Clothing | |
| Groceries/Food | |
| Others | |
| Sub Total | |

Weekly Surplus/Deficit Total: _____

Observations: _____

_____

Changes: _____

_____

22 March - 28 March
# Week 13

Weekly List of Priorities:

## Monday

## Tuesday

## Wednesday

## Thursday

## Friday

## Saturday

## Sunday

*22 March - 28 March*
# Week 13 Finance Record

| *Income* | *Total* |
|---|---|
| Salary or Commissions | |
| Supplemental Income | |
| Sub Total | |
| *Investments* | *Total* |
| Tithes, Offerings, Seeds | |
| Investment Portfolio | |
| Savings Plan / Asue | |
| Sub Total | |
| *Expenditures* | *Total* |
| Mortage/Rent/Utilities | |
| Health, Life & National Ins. | |
| Auto Fuel and Maintenance | |
| Loans, Retirement & Vacations | |
| Entertainment/Clothing | |
| Groceries/Food | |
| Others | |
| Sub Total | |

Weekly Surplus/Deficit Total: _____

Observations: _____

_____

Changes: _____

_____

# March Review

## Achieved

## What can I do better?

Notes:

# April

| Monday | Tuesday | Wednesday | Thursday | Friday | Saturday | Sunday |
|--------|---------|-----------|----------|--------|----------|--------|
|        |         |           | 1        | 2      | 3        | 4      |
| 5      | 6       | 7         | 8        | 9      | 10       | 11     |
| 12     | 13      | 14        | 15       | 16     | 17       | 18     |
| 19     | 20      | 21        | 22       | 23     | 24       | 25     |
| 26     | 27      | 28        | 29       | 30     |          |        |

*Psalm 16:8*

I keep my eyes always on the *Lord.*
With him at my right hand,
**I will not be shaken.**

# April
## To-do List

Item:            Due Date:           Complete

# April Budget

## Income

| | Projected | Actual |
|---|---|---|
| Salary | | |
| Income 2 | | |
| Income 3 | | |
| Totals: | | |

## Expenses

### Gifts & Donations

| | Projected | Actual |
|---|---|---|
| Tithes | | |
| Offerings | | |
| Charity | | |
| Other | | |
| Totals: | | |

### Housing

| | Projected | Actual |
|---|---|---|
| Mortage/Rent | | |
| Maint./Repairs | | |
| Phone/Internet | | |
| BPL | | |
| Water & Sew.. | | |
| Propane Gas | | |
| Home Ins. | | |
| Real Prop. Tax | | |
| Other | | |
| Totals: | | |

## Personal

| | Projected | Actual |
|---|---|---|
| Personal Loans | | |
| Credit Cards | | |
| Retirement Plan | | |
| Savings Plan | | |
| Health Ins. | | |
| Life & Nat. Ins. | | |
| Groceries/Food | | |
| Investments | | |
| Clothing/Cleaning | | |
| Entertainment | | |
| Vacation | | |
| Other | | |
| Totals: | | |

## Transportation

| | Projected | Actual |
|---|---|---|
| Vehicle/Transport | | |
| Car Insurance | | |
| Car Licensing | | |
| Car Maint. | | |
| Fuel Cost | | |
| Other | | |
| Totals: | | |

## Total Expenses

| | Projected | Actual |
|---|---|---|
| Total Expenses: | | |

29 March - 4 April
# Week 14

Weekly List of Priorities:

**Monday**

**Tuesday**

**Wednesday**

**Thursday**

**Friday**

**Saturday**

**Sunday**

*29 March - 4 April*
# Week 14 Finance Record

| *Income* | *Total* |
|---|---|
| Salary or Commissions | |
| Supplemental Income | |
| Sub Total | |
| *Investments* | *Total* |
| Tithes, Offerings, Seeds | |
| Investment Portfolio | |
| Savings Plan / Asue | |
| Sub Total | |
| *Expenditures* | *Total* |
| Mortage/Rent/Utilities | |
| Health, Life & National Ins. | |
| Auto Fuel and Maintenance | |
| Loans, Retirement & Vacations | |
| Entertainment/Clothing | |
| Groceries/Food | |
| Others | |
| Sub Total | |

Weekly Surplus/Deficit Total: _____

Observations: _____

_____

Changes: _____

_____

5 April - 11 April
# Week 15

Weekly List of Priorities:

**Monday**

**Tuesday**

**Wednesday**

**Thursday**

**Friday**

**Saturday**

**Sunday**

*5 April - 11 April*
# Week 15 Finance Record

| Income | Total |
|---|---|
| Salary or Commissions | |
| Supplemental Income | |
| Sub Total | |
| *Investments* | Total |
| Tithes, Offerings, Seeds | |
| Investment Portfolio | |
| Savings Plan / Asue | |
| Sub Total | |
| *Expenditures* | Total |
| Mortage/Rent/Utilities | |
| Health, Life & National Ins. | |
| Auto Fuel and Maintenance | |
| Loans, Retirement & Vacations | |
| Entertainment/Clothing | |
| Groceries/Food | |
| Others | |
| Sub Total | |

Weekly Surplus/Deficit Total: _____

Observations: _____

_____

Changes: _____

_____

12 April - 18 April
# Week 16

Weekly List of Priorities:

### Monday

### Tuesday

### Wednesday

### Thursday

### Friday

### Saturday

### Sunday

*12 April - 18 April*

# Week 16 Finance Record

| *Income* | *Total* |
|---|---|
| Salary or Commissions | |
| Supplemental Income | |
| Sub Total | |

| *Investments* | *Total* |
|---|---|
| Tithes, Offerings, Seeds | |
| Investment Portfolio | |
| Savings Plan / Asue | |
| Sub Total | |

| *Expenditures* | *Total* |
|---|---|
| Mortage/Rent/Utilities | |
| Health, Life & National Ins. | |
| Auto Fuel and Maintenance | |
| Loans, Retirement & Vacations | |
| Entertainment/Clothing | |
| Groceries/Food | |
| Others | |
| Sub Total | |

Weekly Surplus/Deficit Total: _____

Observations: _____

_____

Changes: _____

_____

*19 April - 25 April*
# Week 17

Weekly List of Priorities:

### Monday

### Tuesday

### Wednesday

### Thursday

### Friday

### Saturday

### Sunday

*19 April - 25 April*
# Week 17 Finance Record

| *Income* | | *Total* |
|---|---|---|
| Salary or Commissions | | |
| Supplemental Income | | |
| | Sub Total | |
| *Investments* | | *Total* |
| Tithes, Offerings, Seeds | | |
| Investment Portfolio | | |
| Savings Plan / Asue | | |
| | Sub Total | |
| *Expenditures* | | *Total* |
| Mortage/Rent/Utilities | | |
| Health, Life & National Ins. | | |
| Auto Fuel and Maintenance | | |
| Loans, Retirement & Vacations | | |
| Entertainment/Clothing | | |
| Groceries/Food | | |
| Others | | |
| | Sub Total | |

Weekly Surplus/Deficit Total: _____

Observations: _____

_____

Changes: _____

# April Review

## Achieved

## What can I do better?

Notes:

# May

| Monday | Tuesday | Wednesday | Thursday | Friday | Saturday | Sunday |
|--------|---------|-----------|----------|--------|----------|--------|
|        |         |           |          | 1      | 1        | 2      |
| 3      | 4       | 5         | 6        | 7      | 8        | 9      |
| 10     | 11      | 12        | 13       | 14     | 15       | 16     |
| 17     | 18      | 19        | 20       | 21     | 22       | 23     |
| 24     | 25      | 26        | 27       | 28     | 29       | 30     |
| 31     |         |           |          |        |          |        |

Let us not become weary in doing good, for at the proper time we will **reap a harvest** if we do not give up. *Galatians 6:9*

# May
## To-do List

| Item: | Due Date: | Complete |
|-------|-----------|----------|
|       |           |          |

# May Budget

## Income

| | Projected | Actual |
|---|---|---|
| Salary | | |
| Income 2 | | |
| Income 3 | | |
| Totals: | | |

## Personal

| | Projected | Actual |
|---|---|---|
| Personal Loans | | |
| Credit Cards | | |
| Retirement Plan | | |
| Savings Plan | | |
| Health Ins. | | |
| Life & Nat. Ins. | | |
| Groceries/Food | | |
| Investments | | |
| Clothing/Cleaning | | |
| Entertainment | | |
| Vacation | | |
| Other | | |
| Totals: | | |

## Expenses

### Gifts & Donations

| | Projected | Actual |
|---|---|---|
| Tithes | | |
| Offerings | | |
| Charity | | |
| Other | | |
| Totals: | | |

### Housing

| | Projected | Actual |
|---|---|---|
| Mortage/Rent | | |
| Maint./Repairs | | |
| Phone/Internet | | |
| BPL | | |
| Water & Sew. | | |
| Propane Gas | | |
| Home Ins. | | |
| Real Prop. Tax | | |
| Other | | |
| Totals: | | |

### Transportation

| | Projected | Actual |
|---|---|---|
| Vehicle/Transport | | |
| Car Insurance | | |
| Car Licensing | | |
| Car Maint. | | |
| Fuel Cost | | |
| Other | | |
| Totals: | | |

## Total Expenses

| | Projected | Actual |
|---|---|---|
| Total Expenses: | | |

26 April - 2 May
# Week 18

Weekly List of Priorities:

## Monday

## Tuesday

## Wednesday

## Thursday

## Friday

## Saturday

## Sunday

# 26 April - 2 May
# Week 18 Finance Record

| Income | Total |
|---|---|
| Salary or Commissions | |
| Supplemental Income | |
| Sub Total | |

| Investments | Total |
|---|---|
| Tithes, Offerings, Seeds | |
| Investment Portfolio | |
| Savings Plan / Asue | |
| Sub Total | |

| Expenditures | Total |
|---|---|
| Mortage/Rent/Utilities | |
| Health, Life & National Ins. | |
| Auto Fuel and Maintenance | |
| Loans, Retirement & Vacations | |
| Entertainment/Clothing | |
| Groceries/Food | |
| Others | |
| Sub Total | |

Weekly Surplus/Deficit Total: _____

Observations: _____

Changes: _____

3 May - 9 May
# Week 19

Weekly List of Priorities:

**Monday**

**Tuesday**

**Wednesday**

**Thursday**

**Friday**

**Saturday**

**Sunday**

# 3 May - 9 May
# Week 19 Finance Record

| Income | Total |
|---|---|
| Salary or Commissions | |
| Supplemental Income | |
| Sub Total | |
| *Investments* | Total |
| Tithes, Offerings, Seeds | |
| Investment Portfolio | |
| Savings Plan / Asue | |
| Sub Total | |
| *Expenditures* | Total |
| Mortage/Rent/Utilities | |
| Health, Life & National Ins. | |
| Auto Fuel and Maintenance | |
| Loans, Retirement & Vacations | |
| Entertainment/Clothing | |
| Groceries/Food | |
| Others | |
| Sub Total | |

Weekly Surplus/Deficit Total: _____

Observations: _____

Changes: _____

*10 May - 16 May*
# Week 20

Weekly List of Priorities:

- Monday
- Tuesday
- Wednesday
- Thursday
- Friday
- Saturday
- Sunday

# 10 May - 16 May
# Week 20 Finance Record

| Income | Total |
|---|---|
| Salary or Commissions | |
| Supplemental Income | |
| Sub Total | |
| **Investments** | **Total** |
| Tithes, Offerings, Seeds | |
| Investment Portfolio | |
| Savings Plan / Asue | |
| Sub Total | |
| **Expenditures** | **Total** |
| Mortage/Rent/Utilities | |
| Health, Life & National Ins. | |
| Auto Fuel and Maintenance | |
| Loans, Retirement & Vacations | |
| Entertainment/Clothing | |
| Groceries/Food | |
| Others | |
| Sub Total | |

Weekly Surplus/Deficit Total: _____

Observations: _____

Changes: _____

17 May - 23 May
# Week 21

Weekly List of Priorities:

### Monday

### Tuesday

### Wednesday

### Thursday

### Friday

### Saturday

### Sunday

*17 May - 23 May*
# Week 21 Finance Record

| *Income* | *Total* |
|---|---|
| Salary or Commissions | |
| Supplemental Income | |
| Sub Total | |
| *Investments* | *Total* |
| Tithes, Offerings, Seeds | |
| Investment Portfolio | |
| Savings Plan / Asue | |
| Sub Total | |
| *Expenditures* | *Total* |
| Mortage/Rent/Utilities | |
| Health, Life & National Ins. | |
| Auto Fuel and Maintenance | |
| Loans, Retirement & Vacations | |
| Entertainment/Clothing | |
| Groceries/Food | |
| Others | |
| Sub Total | |

Weekly Surplus/Deficit Total: _____

Observations: _____

Changes: _____

*24 May - 30 May*
# Week 22

Weekly List of Priorities:

- Monday
- Tuesday
- Wednesday
- Thursday
- Friday
- Saturday
- Sunday

# 24 May - 30 May
# Week 22 Finance Record

| Income | Total |
|---|---|
| Salary or Commissions | |
| Supplemental Income | |
| Sub Total | |
| **Investments** | **Total** |
| Tithes, Offerings, Seeds | |
| Investment Portfolio | |
| Savings Plan / Asue | |
| Sub Total | |
| **Expenditures** | **Total** |
| Mortage/Rent/Utilities | |
| Health, Life & National Ins. | |
| Auto Fuel and Maintenance | |
| Loans, Retirement & Vacations | |
| Entertainment/Clothing | |
| Groceries/Food | |
| Others | |
| Sub Total | |

Weekly Surplus/Deficit Total: _____

Observations: _____

_____

Changes: _____

# May Review

## Achieved

## What can I do better?

Notes:

# June

| Monday | Tuesday | Wednesday | Thursday | Friday | Saturday | Sunday |
|---|---|---|---|---|---|---|
|  | 1 | 2 | 3 | 4 | 5 | 6 |
| 7 | 8 | 9 | 10 | 11 | 12 | 13 |
| 14 | 15 | 16 | 17 | 18 | 19 | 20 |
| 21 | 22 | 23 | 24 | 25 | 26 | 27 |
| 28 | 29 | 30 |  |  |  |  |

Therefore, my dear brothers and sisters, **stand firm**. Let nothing move you. Always give yourselves fully to the work of the *Lord*, because you know that labor in the *Lord* is not in vain. *1 Corinthians 15:58*

## To-do List

Item:　　　　　　　　Due Date:　　　　Complete

# June Budget

## Income

| | Projected | Actual |
|---|---|---|
| Salary | | |
| Income 2 | | |
| Income 3 | | |
| Totals: | | |

## Personal

| | Projected | Actual |
|---|---|---|
| Personal Loans | | |
| Credit Cards | | |
| Retirement Plan | | |
| Savings Plan | | |
| Health Ins. | | |
| Life & Nat. Ins. | | |
| Groceries/Food | | |
| Investments | | |
| Clothing/Cleaning | | |
| Entertainment | | |
| Vacation | | |
| Other | | |
| Totals: | | |

## Expenses

### Gifts & Donations

| | Projected | Actual |
|---|---|---|
| Tithes | | |
| Offerings | | |
| Charity | | |
| Other | | |
| Totals: | | |

### Housing

| | Projected | Actual |
|---|---|---|
| Mortage/Rent | | |
| Maint./Repairs | | |
| Phone/Internet | | |
| BPL | | |
| Water & Sew. | | |
| Propane Gas | | |
| Home Ins. | | |
| Real Prop. Tax | | |
| Other | | |
| Totals: | | |

### Transportation

| | Projected | Actual |
|---|---|---|
| Vehicle/Transport | | |
| Car Insurance | | |
| Car Licensing | | |
| Car Maint. | | |
| Fuel Cost | | |
| Other | | |
| Totals: | | |

### Total Expenses

| | Projected | Actual |
|---|---|---|
| Total Expenses: | | |

31 May - 6 June
# Week 23

Weekly List of Priorities:

### Monday

### Tuesday

### Wednesday

### Thursday

### Friday

### Saturday

### Sunday

# 31 May - 6 June
# Week 23 Finance Record

| Income | Total |
|---|---|
| Salary or Commissions | |
| Supplemental Income | |
| Sub Total | |

| Investments | Total |
|---|---|
| Tithes, Offerings, Seeds | |
| Investment Portfolio | |
| Savings Plan / Asue | |
| Sub Total | |

| Expenditures | Total |
|---|---|
| Mortage/Rent/Utilities | |
| Health, Life & National Ins. | |
| Auto Fuel and Maintenance | |
| Loans, Retirement & Vacations | |
| Entertainment/Clothing | |
| Groceries/Food | |
| Others | |
| Sub Total | |

Weekly Surplus/Deficit Total: _____

Observations: _____

_____

Changes: _____

_____

7 June - 13 June
# Week 24

Weekly List of Priorities:

**Monday**

**Tuesday**

**Wednesday**

**Thursday**

**Friday**

**Saturday**

**Sunday**

# 7 June - 13 June
# Week 24 Finance Record

| Income | Total |
|---|---|
| Salary or Commissions | |
| Supplemental Income | |
| Sub Total | |

| Investments | Total |
|---|---|
| Tithes, Offerings, Seeds | |
| Investment Portfolio | |
| Savings Plan / Asue | |
| Sub Total | |

| Expenditures | Total |
|---|---|
| Mortage/Rent/Utilities | |
| Health, Life & National Ins. | |
| Auto Fuel and Maintenance | |
| Loans, Retirement & Vacations | |
| Entertainment/Clothing | |
| Groceries/Food | |
| Others | |
| Sub Total | |

Weekly Surplus/Deficit Total: _____

Observations: _____

_____

Changes: _____

*14 June - 20 June*
# Week 25

Weekly List of Priorities:

## Monday

## Tuesday

## Wednesday

## Thursday

## Friday

## Saturday

## Sunday

*14 June - 20 June*
# Week 25 Finance Record

| *Income* | *Total* |
|---|---|
| Salary or Commissions | |
| Supplemental Income | |
| Sub Total | |
| *Investments* | *Total* |
| Tithes, Offerings, Seeds | |
| Investment Portfolio | |
| Savings Plan / Asue | |
| Sub Total | |
| *Expenditures* | *Total* |
| Mortage/Rent/Utilities | |
| Health, Life & National Ins. | |
| Auto Fuel and Maintenance | |
| Loans, Retirement & Vacations | |
| Entertainment/Clothing | |
| Groceries/Food | |
| Others | |
| Sub Total | |

Weekly Surplus/Deficit Total: _____

Observations: _____

_____

Changes: _____

_____

*21 June - 27 June*
# Week 26

Weekly List of Priorities:

*Monday*

*Tuesday*

*Wednesday*

*Thursday*

*Friday*

*Saturday*

*Sunday*

*21 June - 27 June*
# Week 26 Finance Record

| *Income* | Total |
|---|---|
| Salary or Commissions | |
| Supplemental Income | |
| Sub Total | |

| *Investments* | Total |
|---|---|
| Tithes, Offerings, Seeds | |
| Investment Portfolio | |
| Savings Plan / Asue | |
| Sub Total | |

| *Expenditures* | Total |
|---|---|
| Mortage/Rent/Utilities | |
| Health, Life & National Ins. | |
| Auto Fuel and Maintenance | |
| Loans, Retirement & Vacations | |
| Entertainment/Clothing | |
| Groceries/Food | |
| Others | |
| Sub Total | |

Weekly Surplus/Deficit Total: _____

Observations: _____

_____

Changes: _____

_____

# June Review

## Achieved

## What can I do better?

Notes:

# July

| Monday | Tuesday | Wednesday | Thursday | Friday | Saturday | Sunday |
|--------|---------|-----------|----------|--------|----------|--------|
|        |         |           | 1        | 2      | 3        | 4      |
| 5      | 6       | 7         | 8        | 9      | 10       | 11     |
| 12     | 13      | 14        | 15       | 16     | 17       | 18     |
| 19     | 20      | 21        | 22       | 23     | 24       | 25     |
| 26     | 27      | 28        | 29       | 30     | 31       |        |

Trust in the *Lord* with all your heart;
do not depend on your own understanding.
Seek His will in all you do,
and He will show you which path to take.

*Proverbs 3:5-6*

Item:            Due Date:        Complete

# July Budget

## Income

| | Projected | Actual |
|---|---|---|
| Salary | | |
| Income 2 | | |
| Income 3 | | |
| Totals: | | |

## Personal

| | Projected | Actual |
|---|---|---|
| Personal Loans | | |
| Credit Cards | | |
| Retirement Plan | | |
| Savings Plan | | |
| Health Ins. | | |
| Life & Nat. Ins. | | |
| Groceries/Food | | |
| Investments | | |
| Clothing/Cleaning | | |
| Entertainment | | |
| Vacation | | |
| Other | | |
| Totals: | | |

## Expenses

### Gifts & Donations

| | Projected | Actual |
|---|---|---|
| Tithes | | |
| Offerings | | |
| Charity | | |
| Other | | |
| Totals: | | |

### Housing

| | Projected | Actual |
|---|---|---|
| Mortage/Rent | | |
| Maint./Repairs | | |
| Phone/Internet | | |
| BPL | | |
| Water & Sew. | | |
| Propane Gas | | |
| Home Ins. | | |
| Real Prop. Tax | | |
| Other | | |
| Totals: | | |

### Transportation

| | Projected | Actual |
|---|---|---|
| Vehicle/Transport | | |
| Car Insurance | | |
| Car Licensing | | |
| Car Maint. | | |
| Fuel Cost | | |
| Other | | |
| Totals: | | |

### Total Expenses

| | Projected | Actual |
|---|---|---|
| Total Expenses: | | |

*28 June - 4 July*
# Week 27

Weekly List of Priorities:

*Monday*

*Tuesday*

*Wednesday*

*Thursday*

*Friday*

*Saturday*

*Sunday*

*28 June - 4 July*
# Week 27 Finance Record

| Income | Total |
|---|---|
| Salary or Commissions | |
| Supplemental Income | |
| Sub Total | |
| *Investments* | Total |
| Tithes, Offerings, Seeds | |
| Investment Portfolio | |
| Savings Plan / Asue | |
| Sub Total | |
| *Expenditures* | Total |
| Mortage/Rent/Utilities | |
| Health, Life & National Ins. | |
| Auto Fuel and Maintenance | |
| Loans, Retirement & Vacations | |
| Entertainment/Clothing | |
| Groceries/Food | |
| Others | |
| Sub Total | |

Weekly Surplus/Deficit Total: _____

Observations: _____

_____

Changes: _____

_____

5 July - 11 July
# Week 28

Weekly List of Priorities:

**Monday**

**Tuesday**

**Wednesday**

**Thursday**

**Friday**

**Saturday**

**Sunday**

# 5 July - 11 July
# Week 28 Finance Record

| Income | Total |
|---|---|
| Salary or Commissions | |
| Supplemental Income | |
| Sub Total | |

| Investments | Total |
|---|---|
| Tithes, Offerings, Seeds | |
| Investment Portfolio | |
| Savings Plan / Asue | |
| Sub Total | |

| Expenditures | Total |
|---|---|
| Mortage/Rent/Utilities | |
| Health, Life & National Ins. | |
| Auto Fuel and Maintenance | |
| Loans, Retirement & Vacations | |
| Entertainment/Clothing | |
| Groceries/Food | |
| Others | |
| Sub Total | |

Weekly Surplus/Deficit Total: _____

Observations: _____

_____

Changes: _____

12 July - 18 July
# Week 29

Weekly List of Priorities:

**Monday**

**Tuesday**

**Wednesday**

**Thursday**

**Friday**

**Saturday**

**Sunday**

# 12 July - 18 July
# Week 29 Finance Record

| Income | Total |
|---|---|
| Salary or Commissions | |
| Supplemental Income | |
| Sub Total | |

| Investments | Total |
|---|---|
| Tithes, Offerings, Seeds | |
| Investment Portfolio | |
| Savings Plan / Asue | |
| Sub Total | |

| Expenditures | Total |
|---|---|
| Mortage/Rent/Utilities | |
| Health, Life & National Ins. | |
| Auto Fuel and Maintenance | |
| Loans, Retirement & Vacations | |
| Entertainment/Clothing | |
| Groceries/Food | |
| Others | |
| Sub Total | |

Weekly Surplus/Deficit Total: _____

Observations: _____

Changes: _____

19 July - 25 July
# Week 30

Weekly List of Priorities:

**Monday**

**Tuesday**

**Wednesday**

**Thursday**

**Friday**

**Saturday**

**Sunday**

*19 July - 25 July*
# Week 30 Finance Record

| Income | Total |
|---|---|
| Salary or Commissions | |
| Supplemental Income | |
| Sub Total | |
| *Investments* | Total |
| Tithes, Offerings, Seeds | |
| Investment Portfolio | |
| Savings Plan / Asue | |
| Sub Total | |
| *Expenditures* | Total |
| Mortage/Rent/Utilities | |
| Health, Life & National Ins. | |
| Auto Fuel and Maintenance | |
| Loans, Retirement & Vacations | |
| Entertainment/Clothing | |
| Groceries/Food | |
| Others | |
| Sub Total | |

Weekly Surplus/Deficit Total: _____

Observations: _____

_____

Changes: _____

# July Review

## Achieved

## What can I do better?

## Notes:

# August

| Monday | Tuesday | Wednesday | Thursday | Friday | Saturday | Sunday |
|--------|---------|-----------|----------|--------|----------|--------|
|        |         |           |          |        |          | 1      |
| 2      | 3       | 4         | 5        | 6      | 7        | 8      |
| 9      | 10      | 11        | 12       | 13     | 14       | 15     |
| 16     | 17      | 18        | 19       | 20     | 21       | 22     |
| 23     | 24      | 25        | 26       | 27     | 28       | 29     |
| 30     | 31      |           |          |        |          |        |

May the *God* of hope fill you with all joy and peace as you trust in Him, so that you may overflow with hope by the power of the *Holy Spirit*. *Romans 15:13*

# August
## To-do List

Item:  Due Date:  Complete

# August Budget

## Income

|  | Projected | Actual |
|---|---|---|
| Salary |  |  |
| Income 2 |  |  |
| Income 3 |  |  |
| Totals: |  |  |

## Expenses

### Gifts & Donations

|  | Projected | Actual |
|---|---|---|
| Tithes |  |  |
| Offerings |  |  |
| Charity |  |  |
| Other |  |  |
| Totals: |  |  |

## Personal

|  | Projected | Actual |
|---|---|---|
| Personal Loans |  |  |
| Credit Cards |  |  |
| Retirement Plan |  |  |
| Savings Plan |  |  |
| Health Ins. |  |  |
| Life & Nat. Ins. |  |  |
| Groceries/Food |  |  |
| Investments |  |  |
| Clothing/Cleaning |  |  |
| Entertainment |  |  |
| Vacation |  |  |
| Other |  |  |
| Totals: |  |  |

## Housing

|  | Projected | Actual |
|---|---|---|
| Mortage/Rent |  |  |
| Maint./Repairs |  |  |
| Phone/Internet |  |  |
| BPL |  |  |
| Water & Sew. |  |  |
| Propane Gas |  |  |
| Home Ins. |  |  |
| Real Prop. Tax |  |  |
| Other |  |  |
| Totals: |  |  |

## Transportation

|  | Projected | Actual |
|---|---|---|
| Vehicle/Transport |  |  |
| Car Insurance |  |  |
| Car Licensing |  |  |
| Car Maint. |  |  |
| Fuel Cost |  |  |
| Other |  |  |
| Totals: |  |  |

## Total Expenses

|  | Projected | Actual |
|---|---|---|
| Total Expenses: |  |  |

26 July - 1 August
# Week 31

Weekly List of Priorities:

**Monday**

**Tuesday**

**Wednesday**

**Thursday**

**Friday**

**Saturday**

**Sunday**

*26 July - 1 August*
# Week 31 Finance Record

| *Income* | *Total* |
|---|---|
| Salary or Commissions | |
| Supplemental Income | |
| Sub Total | |
| *Investments* | *Total* |
| Tithes, Offerings, Seeds | |
| Investment Portfolio | |
| Savings Plan / Asue | |
| Sub Total | |
| *Expenditures* | *Total* |
| Mortage/Rent/Utilities | |
| Health, Life & National Ins. | |
| Auto Fuel and Maintenance | |
| Loans, Retirement & Vacations | |
| Entertainment/Clothing | |
| Groceries/Food | |
| Others | |
| Sub Total | |

Weekly Surplus/Deficit Total: _____

Observations: _____

_____

Changes: _____

_____

2 August - 8 August
# Week 32

Weekly List of Priorities:

*Monday*

*Tuesday*

*Wednesday*

*Thursday*

*Friday*

*Saturday*

*Sunday*

## 2 August - 8 August
# Week 32 Finance Record

| Income | Total |
|---|---|
| Salary or Commissions | |
| Supplemental Income | |
| Sub Total | |
| **Investments** | **Total** |
| Tithes, Offerings, Seeds | |
| Investment Portfolio | |
| Savings Plan / Asue | |
| Sub Total | |
| **Expenditures** | **Total** |
| Mortage/Rent/Utilities | |
| Health, Life & National Ins. | |
| Auto Fuel and Maintenance | |
| Loans, Retirement & Vacations | |
| Entertainment/Clothing | |
| Groceries/Food | |
| Others | |
| Sub Total | |

Weekly Surplus/Deficit Total: _____

Observations: _____

_____

Changes: _____

_____

## Week 33
*9 August - 15 August*

Weekly List of Priorities:

- Monday
- Tuesday
- Wednesday
- Thursday
- Friday
- Saturday
- Sunday

## 9 August - 15 August
# Week 33 Finance Record

| Income | Total |
|---|---|
| Salary or Commissions | |
| Supplemental Income | |
| Sub Total | |
| **Investments** | **Total** |
| Tithes, Offerings, Seeds | |
| Investment Portfolio | |
| Savings Plan / Asue | |
| Sub Total | |
| **Expenditures** | **Total** |
| Mortage/Rent/Utilities | |
| Health, Life & National Ins. | |
| Auto Fuel and Maintenance | |
| Loans, Retirement & Vacations | |
| Entertainment/Clothing | |
| Groceries/Food | |
| Others | |
| Sub Total | |

Weekly Surplus/Deficit Total: _____

Observations: _____

_____

Changes: _____

_____

## 16 August - 22 August
# Week 34

Weekly List of Priorities:

**Monday**

**Tuesday**

**Wednesday**

**Thursday**

**Friday**

**Saturday**

**Sunday**

*16 August - 22 August*
# Week 34 Finance Record

| Income | Total |
|---|---|
| Salary or Commissions | |
| Supplemental Income | |
| Sub Total | |
| Investments | Total |
| Tithes, Offerings, Seeds | |
| Investment Portfolio | |
| Savings Plan / Asue | |
| Sub Total | |
| Expenditures | Total |
| Mortage/Rent/Utilities | |
| Health, Life & National Ins. | |
| Auto Fuel and Maintenance | |
| Loans, Retirement & Vacations | |
| Entertainment/Clothing | |
| Groceries/Food | |
| Others | |
| Sub Total | |

Weekly Surplus/Deficit Total: _____

Observations: _____

_____

Changes: _____

_____

# Week 35
*23 August - 29 August*

Weekly List of Priorities:

**Monday**

**Tuesday**

**Wednesday**

**Thursday**

**Friday**

**Saturday**

**Sunday**

*23 August - 29 August*
# Week 35 Finance Record

| *Income* | *Total* |
|---|---|
| Salary or Commissions | |
| Supplemental Income | |
| Sub Total | |
| *Investments* | *Total* |
| Tithes, Offerings, Seeds | |
| Investment Portfolio | |
| Savings Plan / Asue | |
| Sub Total | |
| *Expenditures* | *Total* |
| Mortage/Rent/Utilities | |
| Health, Life & National Ins. | |
| Auto Fuel and Maintenance | |
| Loans, Retirement & Vacations | |
| Entertainment/Clothing | |
| Groceries/Food | |
| Others | |
| Sub Total | |

Weekly Surplus/Deficit Total: _____

Observations: _____

_____

Changes: _____

_____

# August Review

## Achieved

## What can I do better?

Notes:

# September

| Monday | Tuesday | Wednesday | Thursday | Friday | Saturday | Sunday |
|--------|---------|-----------|----------|--------|----------|--------|
|        |         | 1         | 2        | 3      | 4        | 5      |
| 6      | 7       | 8         | 9        | 10     | 11       | 12     |
| 13     | 14      | 15        | 16       | 17     | 18       | 19     |
| 20     | 21      | 22        | 23       | 24     | 25       | 26     |
| 27     | 28      | 29        | 30       |        |          |        |

*Job 22:28*

You will also declare a thing,
And it will be established for you;
So light will shine on your ways.

## To-do List

Item:      Due Date:      Complete

# September Budget

## Income

| | Projected | Actual |
|---|---|---|
| Salary | | |
| Income 2 | | |
| Income 3 | | |
| Totals: | | |

## Expenses

### Gifts & Donations

| | Projected | Actual |
|---|---|---|
| Tithes | | |
| Offerings | | |
| Charity | | |
| Other | | |
| Totals: | | |

### Housing

| | Projected | Actual |
|---|---|---|
| Mortage/Rent | | |
| Maint./Repairs | | |
| Phone/Internet | | |
| BPL | | |
| Water & Sew. | | |
| Propane Gas | | |
| Home Ins. | | |
| Real Prop. Tax | | |
| Other | | |
| Totals: | | |

### Personal

| | Projected | Actual |
|---|---|---|
| Personal Loans | | |
| Credit Cards | | |
| Retirement Plan | | |
| Savings Plan | | |
| Health Ins. | | |
| Life & Nat. Ins. | | |
| Groceries/Food | | |
| Investments | | |
| Clothing/Cleaning | | |
| Entertainment | | |
| Vacation | | |
| Other | | |
| Totals: | | |

### Transportation

| | Projected | Actual |
|---|---|---|
| Vehicle/Transport | | |
| Car Insurance | | |
| Car Licensing | | |
| Car Maint. | | |
| Fuel Cost | | |
| Other | | |
| Totals: | | |

## Total Expenses

| | Projected | Actual |
|---|---|---|
| Total Expenses: | | |

# 30 August - 5 September
# Week 36

Weekly List of Priorities:

- Monday
- Tuesday
- Wednesday
- Thursday
- Friday
- Saturday
- Sunday

*30 August - 5 September*
# Week 36 Finance Record

| *Income* | *Total* |
|---|---|
| Salary or Commissions | |
| Supplemental Income | |
| Sub Total | |
| *Investments* | *Total* |
| Tithes, Offerings, Seeds | |
| Investment Portfolio | |
| Savings Plan / Asue | |
| Sub Total | |
| *Expenditures* | *Total* |
| Mortage/Rent/Utilities | |
| Health, Life & National Ins. | |
| Auto Fuel and Maintenance | |
| Loans, Retirement & Vacations | |
| Entertainment/Clothing | |
| Groceries/Food | |
| Others | |
| Sub Total | |

Weekly Surplus/Deficit Total: _____

Observations: _____

_____

Changes: _____

_____

# 6 September - 12 September
# Week 37

Weekly List of Priorities:

- Monday
- Tuesday
- Wednesday
- Thursday
- Friday
- Saturday
- Sunday

*6 September - 12 September*
# Week 37 Finance Record

| *Income* | *Total* |
|---|---|
| Salary or Commissions | |
| Supplemental Income | |
| Sub Total | |
| *Investments* | *Total* |
| Tithes, Offerings, Seeds | |
| Investment Portfolio | |
| Savings Plan / Asue | |
| Sub Total | |
| *Expenditures* | *Total* |
| Mortage/Rent/Utilities | |
| Health, Life & National Ins. | |
| Auto Fuel and Maintenance | |
| Loans, Retirement & Vacations | |
| Entertainment/Clothing | |
| Groceries/Food | |
| Others | |
| Sub Total | |

Weekly Surplus/Deficit Total: _____

Observations: _____

Changes: _____

# 13 September - 19 September
# Week 38

Weekly List of Priorities:

**Monday**

**Tuesday**

**Wednesday**

**Thursday**

**Friday**

**Saturday**

**Sunday**

## 13 September - 19 September
# Week 38 Finance Record

| Income | Total |
|---|---|
| Salary or Commissions | |
| Supplemental Income | |
| Sub Total | |
| Investments | Total |
| Tithes, Offerings, Seeds | |
| Investment Portfolio | |
| Savings Plan / Asue | |
| Sub Total | |
| Expenditures | Total |
| Mortage/Rent/Utilities | |
| Health, Life & National Ins. | |
| Auto Fuel and Maintenance | |
| Loans, Retirement & Vacations | |
| Entertainment/Clothing | |
| Groceries/Food | |
| Others | |
| Sub Total | |

Weekly Surplus/Deficit Total: _____

Observations: _____

Changes: _____

*20 September - 26 September*
# Week 39

Weekly List of Priorities:

- Monday
- Tuesday
- Wednesday
- Thursday
- Friday
- Saturday
- Sunday

*20 September - 26 September*
# Week 39 Finance Record

| *Income* | *Total* |
|---|---|
| Salary or Commissions | |
| Supplemental Income | |
| Sub Total | |
| *Investments* | *Total* |
| Tithes, Offerings, Seeds | |
| Investment Portfolio | |
| Savings Plan / Asue | |
| Sub Total | |
| *Expenditures* | *Total* |
| Mortage/Rent/Utilities | |
| Health, Life & National Ins. | |
| Auto Fuel and Maintenance | |
| Loans, Retirement & Vacations | |
| Entertainment/Clothing | |
| Groceries/Food | |
| Others | |
| Sub Total | |

Weekly Surplus/Deficit Total: _____

Observations: _____

_____

Changes: _____

_____

# September Review

## Achieved

## What can I do better?

Notes:

# October

| Monday | Tuesday | Wednesday | Thursday | Friday | Saturday | Sunday |
|--------|---------|-----------|----------|--------|----------|--------|
|        |         |           | 1        | 2      | 3        |        |
| 4      | 5       | 6         | 7        | 8      | 9        | 10     |
| 11     | 12      | 13        | 14       | 15     | 16       | 17     |
| 18     | 19      | 20        | 21       | 22     | 23       | 24     |
| 25     | 26      | 27        | 28       | 29     | 30       | 31     |

Consider it pure joy my brothers and sisters, whenever you face trails of many kinds, because you know that the testing of your faith produces perseverance. Let perseverance finish its work so that you may be mature and complete, not lacking anything. *James 1:2-4*

# October
## To-do List

Item:        Due Date:        Complete

# October Budget

## Income

| | Projected | Actual |
|---|---|---|
| Salary | | |
| Income 2 | | |
| Income 3 | | |
| Totals: | | |

## Expenses

### Gifts & Donations

| | Projected | Actual |
|---|---|---|
| Tithes | | |
| Offerings | | |
| Charity | | |
| Other | | |
| Totals: | | |

### Housing

| | Projected | Actual |
|---|---|---|
| Mortage/Rent | | |
| Maint./Repairs | | |
| Phone/Internet | | |
| BPL | | |
| Water & Sew.. | | |
| Propane Gas | | |
| Home Ins. | | |
| Real Prop. Tax | | |
| Other | | |
| Totals: | | |

## Personal

| | Projected | Actual |
|---|---|---|
| Personal Loans | | |
| Credit Cards | | |
| Retirement Plan | | |
| Savings Plan | | |
| Health Ins. | | |
| Life & Nat. Ins. | | |
| Groceries/Food | | |
| Investments | | |
| Clothing/Cleaning | | |
| Entertainment | | |
| Vacation | | |
| Other | | |
| Totals: | | |

### Transportation

| | Projected | Actual |
|---|---|---|
| Vehicle/Transport | | |
| Car Insurance | | |
| Car Licensing | | |
| Car Maint. | | |
| Fuel Cost | | |
| Other | | |
| Totals: | | |

### Total Expenses

| | Projected | Actual |
|---|---|---|
| Total Expenses: | | |

27 September - 3 October
# Week 40

Weekly List of Priorities:

Monday

Tuesday

Wednesday

Thursday

Friday

Saturday

Sunday

# 27 September - 3 October
# Week 40 Finance Record

| Income | Total |
|---|---|
| Salary or Commissions | |
| Supplemental Income | |
| Sub Total | |
| **Investments** | **Total** |
| Tithes, Offerings, Seeds | |
| Investment Portfolio | |
| Savings Plan / Asue | |
| Sub Total | |
| **Expenditures** | **Total** |
| Mortage/Rent/Utilities | |
| Health, Life & National Ins. | |
| Auto Fuel and Maintenance | |
| Loans, Retirement & Vacations | |
| Entertainment/Clothing | |
| Groceries/Food | |
| Others | |
| Sub Total | |

Weekly Surplus/Deficit Total: _____

Observations: _____

Changes: _____

# 4 October - 10 October
## Week 41

Weekly List of Priorities:

**Monday**

**Tuesday**

**Wednesday**

**Thursday**

**Friday**

**Saturday**

**Sunday**

# 4 October - 10 October
# Week 41 Finance Record

| Income | Total |
|---|---|
| Salary or Commissions | |
| Supplemental Income | |
| Sub Total | |

| Investments | Total |
|---|---|
| Tithes, Offerings, Seeds | |
| Investment Portfolio | |
| Savings Plan / Asue | |
| Sub Total | |

| Expenditures | Total |
|---|---|
| Mortage/Rent/Utilities | |
| Health, Life & National Ins. | |
| Auto Fuel and Maintenance | |
| Loans, Retirement & Vacations | |
| Entertainment/Clothing | |
| Groceries/Food | |
| Others | |
| Sub Total | |

Weekly Surplus/Deficit Total: _____

Observations: _____

_____

Changes: _____

*11 October - 17 October*
# Week 42

Weekly List of Priorities:

## Monday

## Tuesday

## Wednesday

## Thursday

## Friday

## Saturday

## Sunday

# 11 October - 17 October
# Week 42 Finance Record

| Income | Total |
|---|---|
| Salary or Commissions | |
| Supplemental Income | |
| Sub Total | |

| Investments | Total |
|---|---|
| Tithes, Offerings, Seeds | |
| Investment Portfolio | |
| Savings Plan / Asue | |
| Sub Total | |

| Expenditures | Total |
|---|---|
| Mortage/Rent/Utilities | |
| Health, Life & National Ins. | |
| Auto Fuel and Maintenance | |
| Loans, Retirement & Vacations | |
| Entertainment/Clothing | |
| Groceries/Food | |
| Others | |
| Sub Total | |

Weekly Surplus/Deficit Total: _____

Observations: _____

Changes: _____

# 18 October - 24 October
# Week 43

Weekly List of Priorities:

**Monday**

**Tuesday**

**Wednesday**

**Thursday**

**Friday**

**Saturday**

**Sunday**

*18 October - 24 October*
# Week 43 Finance Record

| *Income* | *Total* |
|---|---|
| Salary or Commissions | |
| Supplemental Income | |
| Sub Total | |
| *Investments* | *Total* |
| Tithes, Offerings, Seeds | |
| Investment Portfolio | |
| Savings Plan / Asue | |
| Sub Total | |
| *Expenditures* | *Total* |
| Mortage/Rent/Utilities | |
| Health, Life & National Ins. | |
| Auto Fuel and Maintenance | |
| Loans, Retirement & Vacations | |
| Entertainment/Clothing | |
| Groceries/Food | |
| Others | |
| Sub Total | |

Weekly Surplus/Deficit Total: _____

Observations: _____

Changes: _____

25 October - 31 October
# Week 44

Weekly List of Priorities:

**Monday**

**Tuesday**

**Wednesday**

**Thursday**

**Friday**

**Saturday**

**Sunday**

*25 October - 31 October*
# Week 44 Finance Record

| *Income* | *Total* |
|---|---|
| Salary or Commissions | |
| Supplemental Income | |
| Sub Total | |
| *Investments* | *Total* |
| Tithes, Offerings, Seeds | |
| Investment Portfolio | |
| Savings Plan / Asue | |
| Sub Total | |
| *Expenditures* | *Total* |
| Mortage/Rent/Utilities | |
| Health, Life & National Ins. | |
| Auto Fuel and Maintenance | |
| Loans, Retirement & Vacations | |
| Entertainment/Clothing | |
| Groceries/Food | |
| Others | |
| Sub Total | |

Weekly Surplus/Deficit Total: _____

Observations: _____

_____

Changes: _____

_____

# October Review

## Achieved

## What can I do better?

Notes:

# November

| Monday | Tuesday | Wednesday | Thursday | Friday | Saturday | Sunday |
|---|---|---|---|---|---|---|
| 1 | 2 | 3 | 4 | 5 | 6 | 7 |
| 8 | 9 | 10 | 11 | 12 | 13 | 14 |
| 15 | 16 | 17 | 18 | 19 | 20 | 21 |
| 22 | 23 | 24 | 25 | 26 | 27 | 28 |
| 29 | 30 | | | | | |

...being confident of this, that he who began a good work in you will carry it on to completion until the day of *Christ Jesus.*

*Philippians 1:6*

## To-do List

Item:  Due Date:  Complete

# November Budget

## Income

|  | Projected | Actual |
|---|---|---|
| Salary |  |  |
| Income 2 |  |  |
| Income 3 |  |  |
| Totals: |  |  |

## Expenses

### Gifts & Donations

|  | Projected | Actual |
|---|---|---|
| Tithes |  |  |
| Offerings |  |  |
| Charity |  |  |
| Other |  |  |
| Totals: |  |  |

## Personal

|  | Projected | Actual |
|---|---|---|
| Personal Loans |  |  |
| Credit Cards |  |  |
| Retirement Plan |  |  |
| Savings Plan |  |  |
| Health Ins. |  |  |
| Life & Nat. Ins. |  |  |
| Groceries/Food |  |  |
| Investments |  |  |
| Clothing/Cleaning |  |  |
| Entertainment |  |  |
| Vacation |  |  |
| Other |  |  |
| Totals: |  |  |

## Housing

|  | Projected | Actual |
|---|---|---|
| Mortage/Rent |  |  |
| Maint./Repairs |  |  |
| Phone/Internet |  |  |
| BPL |  |  |
| Water & Sew. |  |  |
| Propane Gas |  |  |
| Home Ins. |  |  |
| Real Prop. Tax |  |  |
| Other |  |  |
| Totals: |  |  |

## Transportation

|  | Projected | Actual |
|---|---|---|
| Vehicle/Transport |  |  |
| Car Insurance |  |  |
| Car Licensing |  |  |
| Car Maint. |  |  |
| Fuel Cost |  |  |
| Other |  |  |
| Totals: |  |  |

## Total Expenses

|  | Projected | Actual |
|---|---|---|
| Total Expenses: |  |  |

*1 November - 7 November*
# Week 45

Weekly List of Priorities:

- Monday
- Tuesday
- Wednesday
- Thursday
- Friday
- Saturday
- Sunday

*1 November - 7 November*
# Week 45 Finance Record

| Income | Total |
|---|---|
| Salary or Commissions | |
| Supplemental Income | |
| Sub Total | |
| **Investments** | **Total** |
| Tithes, Offerings, Seeds | |
| Investment Portfolio | |
| Savings Plan / Asue | |
| Sub Total | |
| **Expenditures** | **Total** |
| Mortage/Rent/Utilities | |
| Health, Life & National Ins. | |
| Auto Fuel and Maintenance | |
| Loans, Retirement & Vacations | |
| Entertainment/Clothing | |
| Groceries/Food | |
| Others | |
| Sub Total | |

Weekly Surplus/Deficit Total: _____

Observations: _____

_____

Changes: _____

# 8 November - 14 November
## Week 46

Weekly List of Priorities:

**Monday**

**Tuesday**

**Wednesday**

**Thursday**

**Friday**

**Saturday**

**Sunday**

# 8 November - 14 November
# Week 46 Finance Record

| Income | Total |
|---|---|
| Salary or Commissions | |
| Supplemental Income | |
| Sub Total | |

| Investments | Total |
|---|---|
| Tithes, Offerings, Seeds | |
| Investment Portfolio | |
| Savings Plan / Asue | |
| Sub Total | |

| Expenditures | Total |
|---|---|
| Mortage/Rent/Utilities | |
| Health, Life & National Ins. | |
| Auto Fuel and Maintenance | |
| Loans, Retirement & Vacations | |
| Entertainment/Clothing | |
| Groceries/Food | |
| Others | |
| Sub Total | |

Weekly Surplus/Deficit Total: _____

Observations: _____

Changes: _____

*15 November - 21 November*
# Week 47

Weekly List of Priorities:

- Monday
- Tuesday
- Wednesday
- Thursday
- Friday
- Saturday
- Sunday

# 15 November - 21 November
# Week 47 Finance Record

| Income | Total |
|---|---|
| Salary or Commissions | |
| Supplemental Income | |
| Sub Total | |
| *Investments* | Total |
| Tithes, Offerings, Seeds | |
| Investment Portfolio | |
| Savings Plan / Asue | |
| Sub Total | |
| *Expenditures* | Total |
| Mortage/Rent/Utilities | |
| Health, Life & National Ins. | |
| Auto Fuel and Maintenance | |
| Loans, Retirement & Vacations | |
| Entertainment/Clothing | |
| Groceries/Food | |
| Others | |
| Sub Total | |

Weekly Surplus/Deficit Total: _____

Observations: _____

Changes: _____

*22 November - 28 November*
# Week 48

Weekly List of Priorities:

- Monday
- Tuesday
- Wednesday
- Thursday
- Friday
- Saturday
- Sunday

## 22 November - 28 November
# Week 48 Finance Record

| Income | Total |
|---|---|
| Salary or Commissions | |
| Supplemental Income | |
| Sub Total | |

| Investments | Total |
|---|---|
| Tithes, Offerings, Seeds | |
| Investment Portfolio | |
| Savings Plan / Asue | |
| Sub Total | |

| Expenditures | Total |
|---|---|
| Mortage/Rent/Utilities | |
| Health, Life & National Ins. | |
| Auto Fuel and Maintenance | |
| Loans, Retirement & Vacations | |
| Entertainment/Clothing | |
| Groceries/Food | |
| Others | |
| Sub Total | |

Weekly Surplus/Deficit Total: _____

Observations: _____

_____

Changes: _____

_____

# November Review

## Achieved

## What can I do better?

## Notes:

# December

| Monday | Tuesday | Wednesday | Thursday | Friday | Saturday | Sunday |
|---|---|---|---|---|---|---|
|  |  | 1 | 2 | 3 | 4 | 5 |
| 6 | 7 | 8 | 9 | 10 | 11 | 12 |
| 13 | 14 | 15 | 16 | 17 | 18 | 19 |
| 20 | 21 | 22 | 23 | 24 | 25 | 26 |
| 27 | 28 | 29 | 30 | 31 |  |  |

*Psalm 46:1-3*

*God* is our refuge and strength, always ready to help in times of trouble. So we will not fear when earthquakes come and the mountains crumble into the sea. Let the oceans roar and foam. Let the mountains tremble as the waters surge!

Item:            Due Date:        Complete

# December Budget

## Income

|  | Projected | Actual |
|---|---|---|
| Salary |  |  |
| Income 2 |  |  |
| Income 3 |  |  |
| Totals: |  |  |

## Expenses

### Gifts & Donations

|  | Projected | Actual |
|---|---|---|
| Tithes |  |  |
| Offerings |  |  |
| Charity |  |  |
| Other |  |  |
| Totals: |  |  |

### Housing

|  | Projected | Actual |
|---|---|---|
| Mortage/Rent |  |  |
| Maint./Repairs |  |  |
| Phone/Internet |  |  |
| BPL |  |  |
| Water & Sew. |  |  |
| Propane Gas |  |  |
| Home Ins. |  |  |
| Real Prop. Tax |  |  |
| Other |  |  |
| Totals: |  |  |

### Personal

|  | Projected | Actual |
|---|---|---|
| Personal Loans |  |  |
| Credit Cards |  |  |
| Retirement Plan |  |  |
| Savings Plan |  |  |
| Health Ins. |  |  |
| Life & Nat. Ins. |  |  |
| Groceries/Food |  |  |
| Investments |  |  |
| Clothing/Cleaning |  |  |
| Entertainment |  |  |
| Vacation |  |  |
| Other |  |  |
| Totals: |  |  |

### Transportation

|  | Projected | Actual |
|---|---|---|
| Vehicle/Transport |  |  |
| Car Insurance |  |  |
| Car Licensing |  |  |
| Car Maint. |  |  |
| Fuel Cost |  |  |
| Other |  |  |
| Totals: |  |  |

### Total Expenses

|  | Projected | Actual |
|---|---|---|
| Total Expenses: |  |  |

*29 November - 5 December*
# Week 49

Weekly List of Priorities:

- Monday
- Tuesday
- Wednesday
- Thursday
- Friday
- Saturday
- Sunday

*29 November - 5 December*
# Week 49 Finance Record

| Income | Total |
|---|---|
| Salary or Commissions | |
| Supplemental Income | |
| Sub Total | |
| *Investments* | *Total* |
| Tithes, Offerings, Seeds | |
| Investment Portfolio | |
| Savings Plan / Asue | |
| Sub Total | |
| *Expenditures* | *Total* |
| Mortage/Rent/Utilities | |
| Health, Life & National Ins. | |
| Auto Fuel and Maintenance | |
| Loans, Retirement & Vacations | |
| Entertainment/Clothing | |
| Groceries/Food | |
| Others | |
| Sub Total | |

Weekly Surplus/Deficit Total: _____

Observations: _____

_____

Changes: _____

_____

# 6 December - 12 December
## Week 50

Weekly List of Priorities:

**Monday**

**Tuesday**

**Wednesday**

**Thursday**

**Friday**

**Saturday**

**Sunday**

# 6 December - 12 December
# Week 50 Finance Record

| Income | Total |
|---|---|
| Salary or Commissions | |
| Supplemental Income | |
| Sub Total | |

| Investments | Total |
|---|---|
| Tithes, Offerings, Seeds | |
| Investment Portfolio | |
| Savings Plan / Asue | |
| Sub Total | |

| Expenditures | Total |
|---|---|
| Mortage/Rent/Utilities | |
| Health, Life & National Ins. | |
| Auto Fuel and Maintenance | |
| Loans, Retirement & Vacations | |
| Entertainment/Clothing | |
| Groceries/Food | |
| Others | |
| Sub Total | |

Weekly Surplus/Deficit Total: _____

Observations: _____

_____

Changes: _____

_____

13 December - 19 December
# Week 51

Weekly List of Priorities:

**Monday**

**Tuesday**

**Wednesday**

**Thursday**

**Friday**

**Saturday**

**Sunday**

*13 December - 19 December*
# Week 51 Finance Record

| *Income* | *Total* |
|---|---|
| Salary or Commissions | |
| Supplemental Income | |
| Sub Total | |
| *Investments* | *Total* |
| Tithes, Offerings, Seeds | |
| Investment Portfolio | |
| Savings Plan / Asue | |
| Sub Total | |
| *Expenditures* | *Total* |
| Mortage/Rent/Utilities | |
| Health, Life & National Ins. | |
| Auto Fuel and Maintenance | |
| Loans, Retirement & Vacations | |
| Entertainment/Clothing | |
| Groceries/Food | |
| Others | |
| Sub Total | |

Weekly Surplus/Deficit Total: _____

Observations: _____

Changes: _____

27 December - 31 December
# Week 53

Weekly List of Priorities:

**Monday**

**Tuesday**

**Wednesday**

**Thursday**

**Friday**

"For I know the plans I have for you," declares the *Lord*, "plans to prosper you and not to harm you, plans to give you hope and a future."

*Jeremiah 29:11*

# 27 December - 31 December
# Week 53 Finance Record

| Income | Total |
|---|---|
| Salary or Commissions | |
| Supplemental Income | |
| Sub Total | |
| Investments | Total |
| Tithes, Offerings, Seeds | |
| Investment Portfolio | |
| Savings Plan / Asue | |
| Sub Total | |
| Expenditures | Total |
| Mortage/Rent/Utilities | |
| Health, Life & National Ins. | |
| Auto Fuel and Maintenance | |
| Loans, Retirement & Vacations | |
| Entertainment/Clothing | |
| Groceries/Food | |
| Others | |
| Sub Total | |

Weekly Surplus/Deficit Total: _____

Observations: _____

_____

Changes: _____

_____

# December Review

## Achieved

## What can I do better?

Notes:

# End of Year Review

## Achieved

## What I learnt this year...

## What can I do better?

*2022...*

# Resources

Name:
Business Name:
Description:
Email:
Telephone:
Website:

Name:
Business Name:
Description:
Email:
Telephone:
Website:

Name:
Business Name:
Description:
Email:
Telephone:
Website:

Name:
Business Name:
Description:
Email:
Telephone:
Website:

Name:
Business Name:
Description:
Email:
Telephone:
Website:

# Resources

Name:
Business Name:
Description:
Email:
Telephone:
Website:

Name:
Business Name:
Description:
Email:
Telephone:
Website:

Name:
Business Name:
Description:
Email:
Telephone:
Website:

Name:
Business Name:
Description:
Email:
Telephone:
Website:

Name:
Business Name:
Description:
Email:
Telephone:
Website:

Made in the USA
Columbia, SC
17 February 2021